piano • vocal • guitar

THE BEATLES

ISBN 0-634-03023-X

HAL•LEONARD®
CORPORATION

7777 W. BLUEMOUND RD. P.O. BOX 13819 MILWAUKEE, WI 53213

Visit Hal Leonard Online at
www.halleonard.com

CONTENTS

LOVE ME DO

Words and Music by JOHN LENNON
and PAUL McCARTNEY

FROM ME TO YOU

Words and Music by JOHN LENNON
and PAUL McCARTNEY

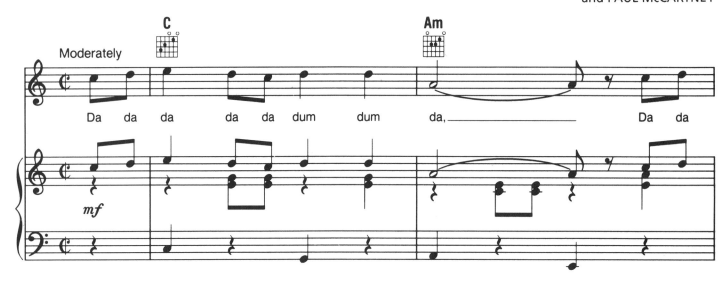

Da da da da da dum dum da,_____ Da da

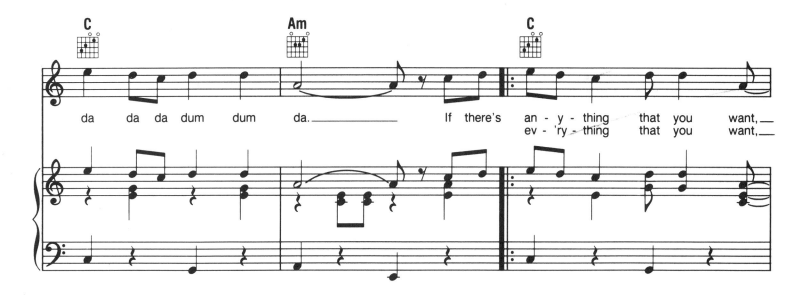

da da da dum dum da._____ If there's an - y - thing that you want,_____
ev - 'ry - thing that you want,_____

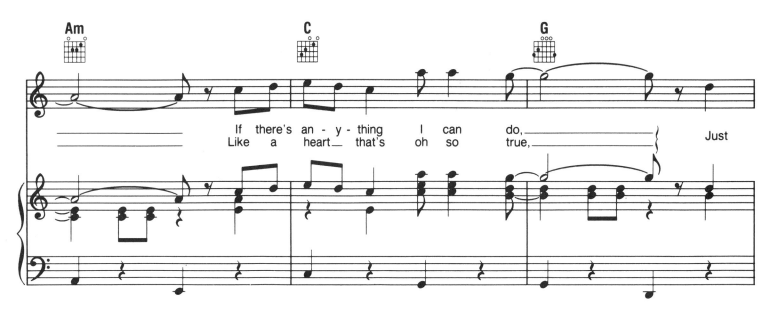

_____ If there's an - y - thing I can do,_____ Just
_____ Like a heart____ that's oh so true,_____

SHE LOVES YOU

Words and Music by JOHN LENNON
and PAUL McCARTNEY

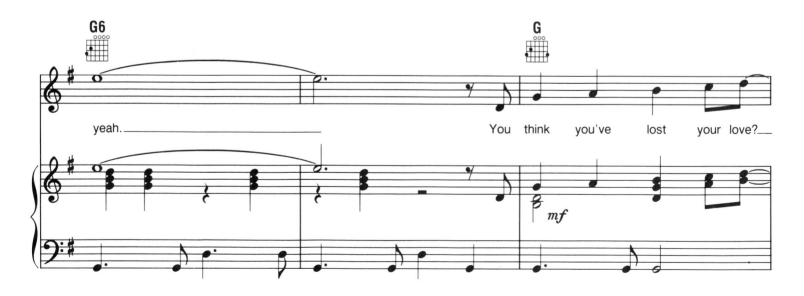

14

I WANT TO HOLD YOUR HAND

Words and Music by JOHN LENNON
and PAUL McCARTNEY

CAN'T BUY ME LOVE

Words and Music by JOHN LENNON
and PAUL McCARTNEY

23

A HARD DAY'S NIGHT

Words and Music by JOHN LENNON
and PAUL McCARTNEY

I FEEL FINE

Words and Music by JOHN LENNON
and PAUL McCARTNEY

EIGHT DAYS A WEEK

Words and Music by JOHN LENNON
and PAUL McCARTNEY

TICKET TO RIDE

Words and Music by JOHN LENNON
and PAUL McCARTNEY

HELP!

Words and Music by JOHN LENNON
and PAUL McCARTNEY

YESTERDAY

Words and Music by JOHN LENNON
and PAUL McCARTNEY

Moderately, with expression

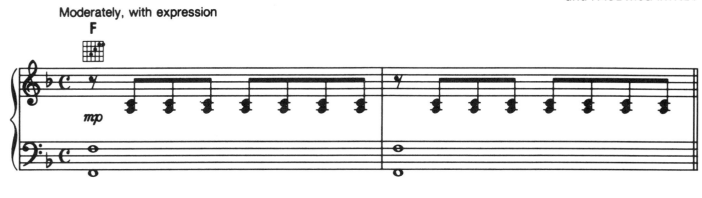

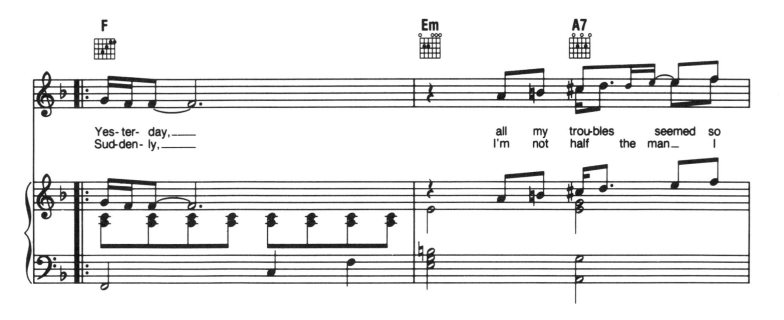

Yes-ter-day,___ all my trou-bles seemed so
Sud-den-ly,___ I'm not half the man___ I

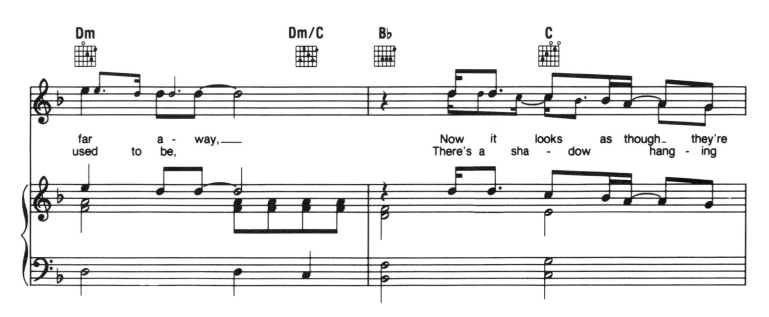

far a-way,___ Now it looks as though___ they're
used to be, There's a sha-dow hang-ing

DAY TRIPPER

Words and Music by JOHN LENNON
and PAUL McCARTNEY

Got a good rea-son
She's a big tea-ser,
Tried to please her,

for

WE CAN WORK IT OUT

Words and Music by JOHN LENNON
and PAUL McCARTNEY

53

54

PAPERBACK WRITER

Words and Music by JOHN LENNON
and PAUL McCARTNEY

Bright Rock

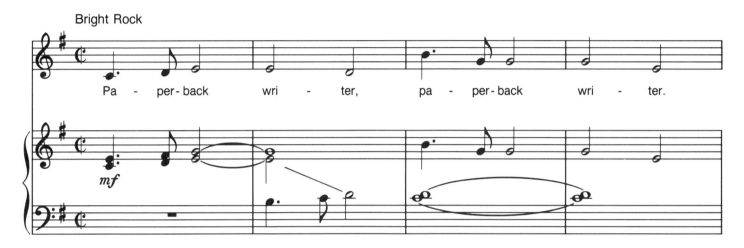

Pa - per - back wri - ter, pa - per - back wri - ter.

G7

Dear__ Sir or Mad - am will you read my book? It took me
It's a thou - sand pag - es, give or take a few; I'll be

58

YELLOW SUBMARINE

Words and Music by JOHN LENNON
and PAUL McCARTNEY

Chorus:

ELEANOR RIGBY

Words and Music by JOHN LENNON
and PAUL McCARTNEY

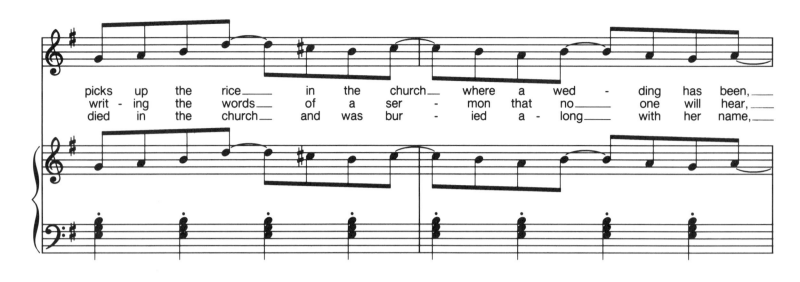

picks up the rice____ in the church____ where a wed - ding has been,____
writ - ing the words____ of a ser - mon that no____ one will hear,____
died in the church____ and was bur - ied a - long____ with her name,____

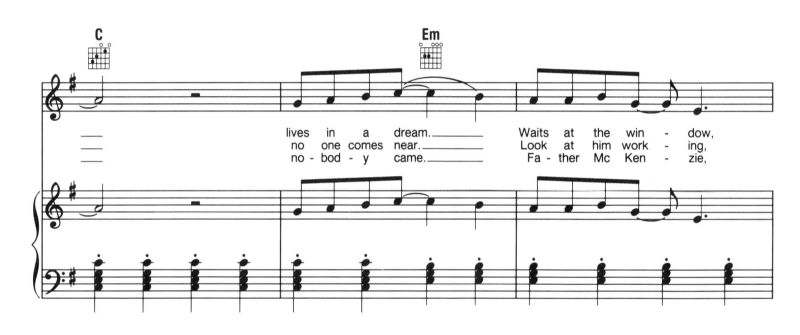

C
Em

____ lives in a dream.____ Waits at the win - dow,
____ no one comes near.____ Look at him work - ing,
____ no - bod - y came.____ Fa - ther Mc Ken - zie,

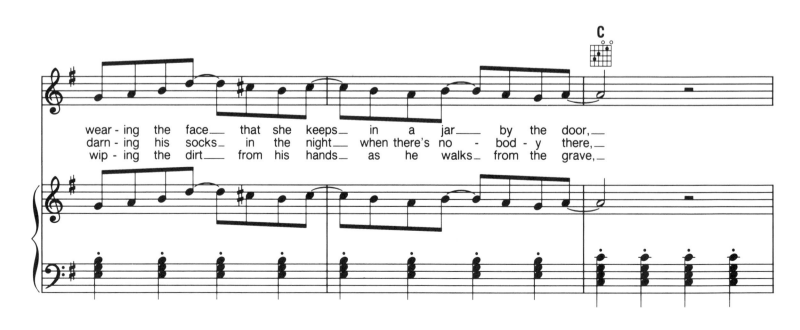

C

wear - ing the face____ that she keeps____ in a jar____ by the door,____
darn - ing his socks____ in the night____ when there's no - bod - y there,____
wip - ing the dirt____ from his hands____ as he walks____ from the grave,____

PENNY LANE

Words and Music by JOHN LENNON
and PAUL McCARTNEY

70

All You Need Is Love

Words and Music by JOHN LENNON
and PAUL McCARTNEY

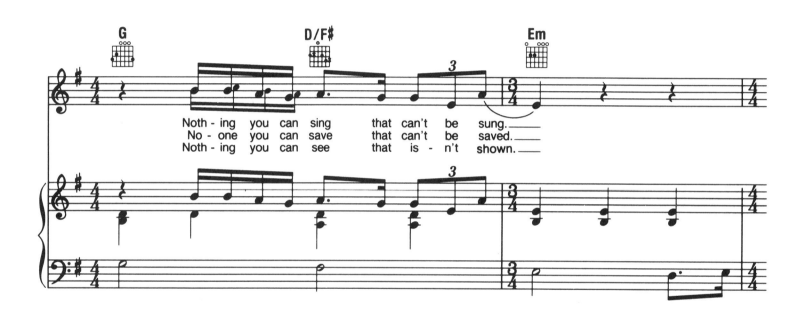

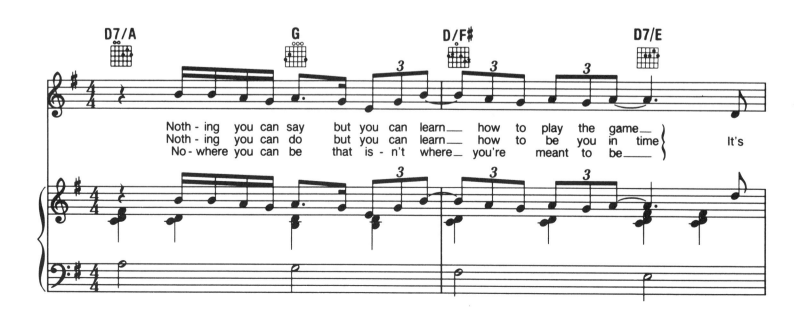

74

HELLO, GOODBYE

Words and Music by JOHN LENNON
and PAUL McCARTNEY

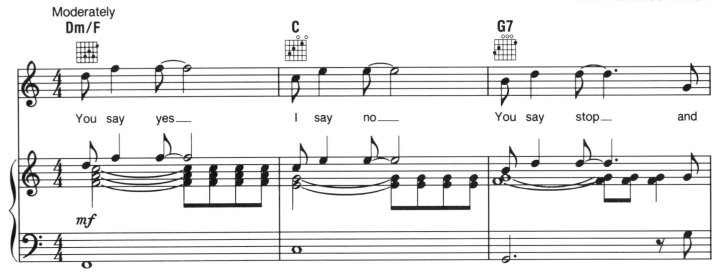

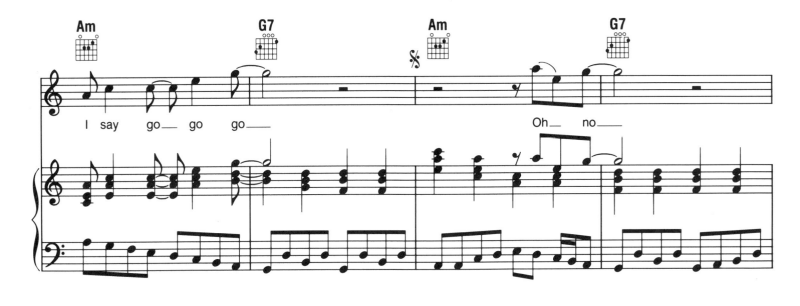

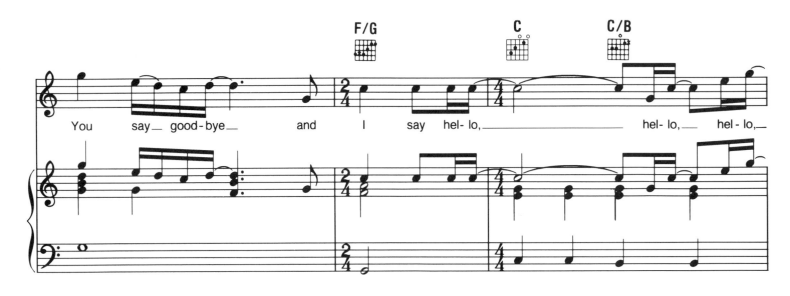

LADY MADONNA

Words and Music by JOHN LENNON
and PAUL McCARTNEY

Brightly, with a beat

A
La - dy Ma - don - na, chil - dren at your feet,
La - dy Ma - don - na, ba - by at your breast,
La - dy Ma - don - na, ly - ing on the bed,
La - dy Ma - don - na, chil - dren at your feet,

D **A** **D**
Won - der how you man - age to make
Won - ders how you man - age to feed
Lis - ten to the mu - sic play - ing
Won - der how you man - age to make

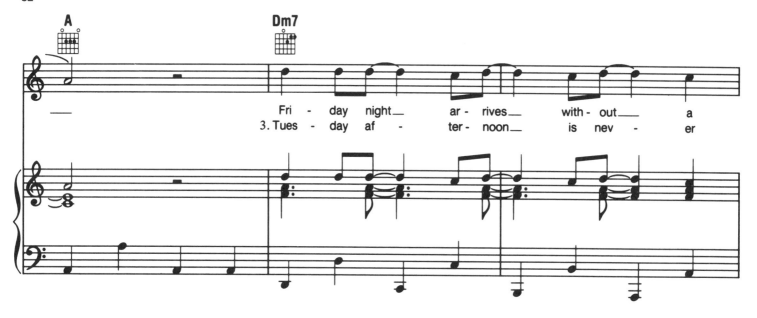

83

HEY JUDE

Words and Music by JOHN LENNON
and PAUL McCARTNEY

GET BACK

Words and Music by JOHN LENNON
and PAUL McCARTNEY

Jo Jo was a man who thought he was a lon-er, But he knew it could-n't last. Jo Jo left his home in Tuc-son Ar-i-zo-na, for some Cal-i-for-nia grass. Get back!

Sweet Lor-et-ta Mar-tin thought she was a wom-an, But she was an-oth-er man. All the girls a-round her say she's got it com-ing, But she gets it while she can.

Instrumental

89

THE BALLAD OF JOHN AND YOKO

Words and Music by JOHN LENNON
and PAUL McCARTNEY

N

91

SOMETHING

Words and Music by
GEORGE HARRISON

Slowly

Some- thing in___ the way___ she moves,___
Some- where in___ her smile___ she knows,___
Some- thing in___ the way___ she knows,___

at- tracts me like___ no oth- er lov- er.
that I___ don't need___ no oth- er lov- er.
and all___ I have to do is think___ of her.

Some- thing in___ the way___ she woos___ me.
Some- thing in___ her style___ that shows___ me.
Some- thing in___ the things___ she shows___ me.

I don't want to leave___ her now, you

COME TOGETHER

Words and Music by JOHN LENNON
and PAUL McCARTNEY

Moderately slow, with a double-time feeling

Here come old flat-top, He come groov-ing up slow-ly, He got Joo Joo eye-ball, He one

ho- ly roll-er, He got hair down to his knee.

Got to be a jok-er, He just do what he please.

Dm7

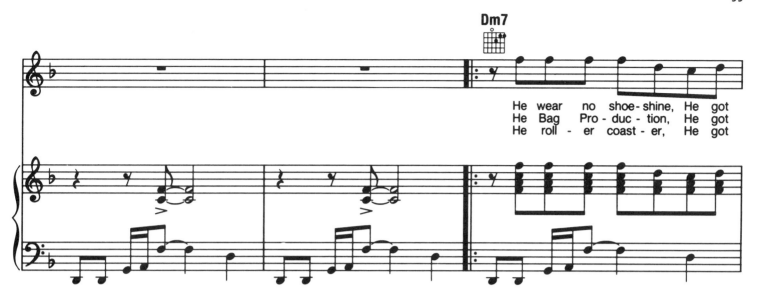

He wear no shoe - shine, He got
He Bag Pro - duc - tion, He got
He roll - er coast - er, He got

toe - jam foot - ball, He got mon - key fin - ger, He shoot Co - ca Co - la; He say,
wal - rus gum - boot, He got O - no side-board, He one spi - nal crack - er, He got
ear - ly warn - ing, He got Mud - dy Wa - ter, He one Mo - jo fil - ter, He say,

A   **G7**   no chord

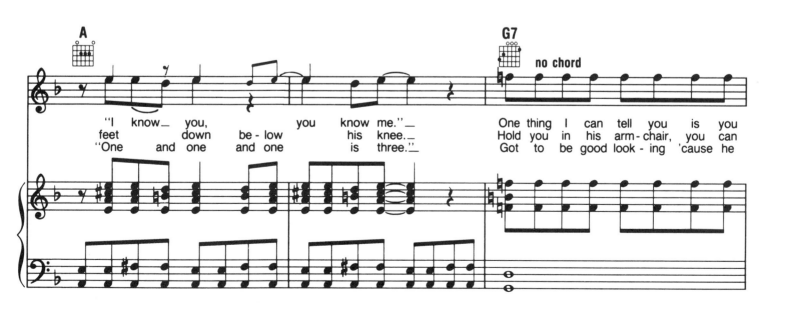

"I know— you,   you know me."— One thing I can tell you is you
feet down be - low his knee.— Hold you in his arm - chair, you can
"One and one and one is three." Got to be good look - ing 'cause he

LET IT BE

Words and Music by JOHN LENNON
and PAUL McCARTNEY

THE LONG AND WINDING ROAD

Words and Music by JOHN LENNON
and PAUL McCARTNEY

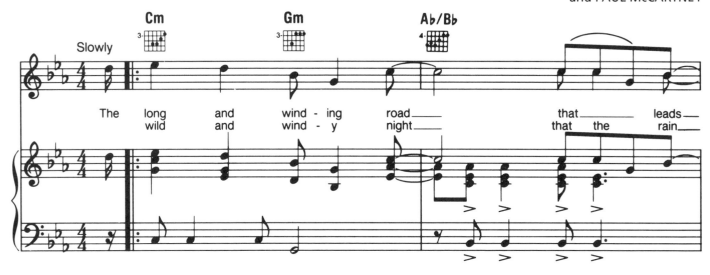

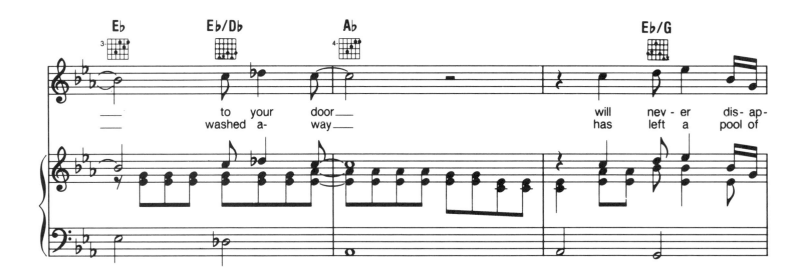

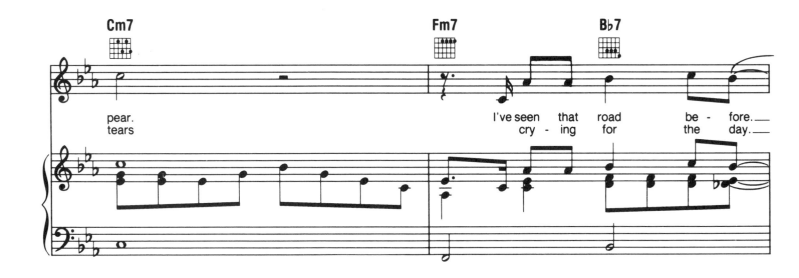

109